Celebrate Philippians
participant guide

Copyright © 2010 by Wesleyan Publishing House
Published by Wesleyan Publishing House
Indianapolis, Indiana 46250
Printed in the United States of America
ISBN: 978-0-89827-452-3

All Scripture quotations, unless otherwise indicated, are taken from the HOLY BIBLE, NEW INTERNATIONAL VERSION ®. NIV ®. Copyright 1973, 1978, 1984 by the International Bible Society. Used by permission of Zondervan. All rights reserved.

Scripture quotations marked (NASB) are taken from the *New American Standard Bible*®, Copyright © 1960, 1962, 1963, 1968, 1971, 1972, 1973, 1975, 1977, 1995 by The Lockman Foundation. Used by permission.

Scripture quotations marked (NLT) are taken from the *Holy Bible, New Living Translation*, copyright 1996, 2004. Used by permission of Tyndale House Publishers, Inc., Wheaton, Illinois 60189. All rights reserved.

Scriptures marked as (CEV) are taken from the *Contemporary English Version* Copyright © 1995 by American Bible Society. Used by permission.

Scripture quotations marked (ESV) are from The Holy Bible, English Standard Version®, copyright © 2001 by Crossway Bibles, a publishing ministry of Good News Publishers. Used by permission. All rights reserved.

Scripture quotation marked (GNT) are taken from the Good News Translation—Second Edition, Copyright 1992 by American Bible Society. Used by Permission.

Scripture quotations marked (MSG) are taken from *The Message*. Copyright © 1993, 1994, 1995, 1996, 2000, 2001, 2002. Used by permission of NavPress Publishing Group.

Scripture quotations marked (NCV) are taken from the New Century Version. Copyright © 2005 by Thomas Nelson, Inc. Used by permission. All rights reserved.

Scripture quotations marked (TNIV) taken from the HOLY BIBLE, TODAY'S NEW INTERNATIONAL VERSION®. Copyright © 2001, 2005 by International Bible Society®. Used by permission of International Bible Society®. All rights reserved worldwide.

All rights reserved. No part of this publication may be reproduced, stored in a retrieval system, or transmitted in any form or by any means—electronic, mechanical, photocopy, recording or any other—except for brief quotations in printed reviews, without the prior written permission of the publisher.

Contents

	Celebrate Series Overview	4
	Study Preview	5
	Guidelines for Group Facilitators	7
1.	Joyful Letter from a Loving Friend	9
2.	Joyfully Exalting Christ	15
3.	Living in Joyful Relationship	21
4.	The King Becomes the Joyful Servant	27
5.	God's Work, the Believer's Work	33
6.	Joyfully Blameless, Living among Scoffers	39
7.	Joy in Loss and Loss in Gain	45
8.	Joy in Running to Win	51
9.	Joy Encircled in God's Protection	57
10.	Joyfully Satisfied in Christ	63
11.	The Joy of Sharing Generously	69
12.	Joy in God's Rich Supply	75

Celebrate Series Overview

The *Celebrate Philippians* DVD and participant guide are part of a series of studies aimed to help people study and apply God's word and experience life transformation. Lessons are designed to be used in small groups but can easily be adapted for individual study.

The DVDs in this series feature the Bible teaching of Pastor Keith Loy. In each study, Pastor Loy will walk you through a book or books from the Bible, with a focus on helping you apply what you learn in a practical way.

Each participant guide contains study notes, as well as additional material to help you process and apply the teaching on the DVD. These include ideas for group sharing, connecting, and discussing, as well as action steps you can follow to implement your learning. You'll also find helpful instructions and guidelines for those who are facilitating small groups.

As you *Celebrate* and study the Word, whether as an individual or in a group, may God richly bless your life and help you grow in knowledge and obedience to our Lord Jesus Christ.

Study Preview

Historic Route 66 meandered through tedious midwestern flatlands, forded rushing rivers, and rose to high altitudes through the Rocky Mountains. One of the beauties of the highway was that it never was meant to be a straight line from Chicago, Illinois, to Santa Monica, California. The journey, which was peppered with roadside stops, diverted around gargantuan obstacles. At times, the road took drivers a day's journey north, when they probably wanted to travel south. At other times, drivers would be desperate for an oasis as they passed through the arid sands of New Mexico and Arizona. Yet, the route rewarded patient drivers who stuck with the two-lane pavement through day upon day of travel with a toe-dip in the majestic Pacific.

In a similar way, the road to joy, as laid out by Paul in his loving letter to the Philippians, will take us in directions we would never have imagined—and frankly, might not want to go. It will call on us to make sacrifices of personal rights to pursue holiness. It will require roadside stops for reconciliation, refreshment, and redirection that we might have thought unnecessary. It will send us down barely paved ways and roads less travelled that seem like detours and possible dead ends. Yet, when we scrutinize the journey

Study Preview

from the other side, we'll see the pathway had a purpose, and that every experience we had along the way helped us draw closer to the one we follow and in whom we find our joy.

In this DVD study of Philippians, you will

- gain a deeper appreciation for what God values (your coming to know him intimately and your relentless pursuit of the prize of his high calling);
- come to understand how God is at work beside you, equipping you to conform you into his son's image; and
- become a more passionate and focused believer who relishes the eternal joy of relationship with him.

As you work your way through these twelve lessons individually or as a group, may you be among those who "may be able to discern what is best and may be pure and blameless until the day of Christ, filled with the fruit of righteousness that comes through Jesus Christ—to the glory and praise of God" (Phil. 1:10–11).

Guidelines for Group Facilitators

This DVD Bible study is designed as a *plug-and-play* small group experience, with little or no preparation necessary prior to each session. However, you'll find it helpful for your group to have a facilitator, someone who will manage details and guide the group's experience. Here are some helpful tips for those who serve as group facilitators.

SET THE ATMOSPHERE

Small groups should be casual, welcoming, and inclusive. Arrange a meeting place where people will feel comfortable and relaxed. Most often, this will be a group member's home, but it could also be a room in your church building that is specially equipped for this kind of meeting. Providing coffee, other beverages, and snacks can also contribute to a relaxed atmosphere.

ENCOURAGE PARTICIPATION

Make sure everyone has the opportunity to participate fully in your group. Each week invite, different people to pray or read or provide refreshments. Also, be ready to give instructions like, "This time let's hear from someone who hasn't spoken up yet," or "Jason, I'm wondering what you're thinking about this. Anything you'd like to share?"

KEEP ON SCHEDULE

This DVD Bible study is designed to take no more than ninety minutes for each session. Here is a typical schedule:

Welcome and Prayer	5 minutes
Share	10 minutes
Connect	15–20 minutes
Discover	10 minutes
Discuss	25–30 minutes
Implement	5–10 minutes
Wrap Up	5 minutes

As facilitator, guide your group through each step of the process and make sure they stay on track and on schedule.

Try to keep your meetings as positive as possible. Establish ground rules early on so that each person in your group is treated with kindness and respect.

Being a group facilitator does require a bit of extra time, but your servant leadership can make a big difference in the overall experience of the group.

Joyful Letter from a Loving Friend

SESSION ONE

PHILIPPIANS 1:1–11

WELCOME and PRAYER
(5 minutes)

SHARE
(10 minutes)

Take turns sharing what you hope to gain from this experience.

CONNECT
(15–20 minutes)

She didn't have the best relationship with her mother. She couldn't recall ever hearing the elder woman say, "I love you."

On her twenty-fifth birthday she received a gold-wrapped package in the mail. It was postmarked with a return address from an exclusive jewelry store in her mother's town. After looking at the package on her desk all day, she finally broke the seal.

Inside the silk-lined box she found a locket. Clicking it open, she saw two pictures: one of herself as a child and the other of her mother in her thirties. She snapped it closed with ambivalence. Then her fingertips ran across something rough. Flipping it over, she read the engraving, "I have you in my heart." And she wept.

Facilitator: Invite group members to participate in the following discussion.

Share with the group the name of one person who needs to hear you say you have him or her in your heart. Maybe it is the person who led you to faith in Christ. Or it may be someone who supported you in a time when you felt all alone, or a family member you don't see often.

DISCOVER
(10 minutes)

Complete the study notes as you watch the DVD together.

Philippians has two major themes. First, it's _____. Second, it's _____.

Paul and the Philippians shared a _____ _____ for one another.

The word *saint* means to be _____ _____ , to be _____.

Philippians 1:1–11

Paul is bringing to the forefront the very _____ and _____ we all have in being a follower of Christ.

_____ is one of the great attributes of the Christian.

Paul is talking about the _____ we have in making sure the _____ of Christ is being _____.

God always _____ what he _____.

The Greek word for *affection* is where we get the word for _____. Paul is saying that his _____ was flowing from the very _____ of who he was.

> Paul challenges us to place our ultimate confidence in God's faithfulness and unchanging nature. This is consistent with Paul's statement to the Roman believers that he is absolutely certain nothing can come between us and the love God shows to us in Christ (Rom. 8:38–39).

God's love _____.

First, he prayed that our love would _____.

Second, Paul prayed that our love would be _____ and _____.

Third, Paul prays for us in _____ we _____.

> *Sincerity is one of the elements of God's prayer for the Philippians. The word carries with it the idea of living with pure motives. Related words are genuine, truth, purity, and godliness.*

Paul's final prayer was, "May you _____ be filled with the _____ of your _____" (Phil 1:11 NLT).

_____ is the by-product of a *pure* and *blameless* _____.

DISCUSS
(25–30 minutes)

1. If Paul were writing this letter to you, what evidence might he see in your spiritual life that would cause him to express thankfulness to God? How do you suppose Paul's original readers felt when they received these tender words? What leads you to believe that they returned Paul's loving affection?

2. Think of at least one person who has stood with you in defense of the gospel. What were the circumstances? With whom have you stood while they were being pressed or challenged for the sake of Christ?

3. Paul prayed for believers to have love full of knowledge and insight. How is biblical love tied to knowledge and insight? When have you seen love grow as you gained knowledge about someone you love?

Philippians 1:1–11

4. Compare Paul's list of spiritual fruit in Galatians 5:22–23 with his reference to the "fruit of righteousness" here in Philippians 1:10–11. What connection does bearing fruit that brings praise to God have with your personal purity and blamelessness? Conversely, what effect does personal impurity or sin have on the fruit you bear for Christ? Why do you suppose Paul ties these concepts so closely together?

> Regarding Paul's prayer for believers to abound in "knowledge and all discernment," Albert Barnes wrote, "The idea is that he wished them to have intelligent affection. It should not be mere blind affection, but that intelligent love which is based on an enlarged view of Divine things— on a just apprehension of the claims of God."

5. In what ways would you like to mature in your faith so Christ himself would be joyful when he looks at the fruit of your life?

IMPLEMENT
(5–10 minutes)

Choose at least one activity to do before the next session. Tell one other person which item you chose.

1. Begin each day this week by re-reading Paul's prayer in Philippians 1:9–11. Choose a loved one for whom you will pray that prayer every day. Jot down notes as you begin to see God answer your prayer.

2. Make time to write notes to the people closest to you just to tell them you have them in your heart. Send the notes by postal mail, e-mail, or text message.

3. During a quiet time with God, express to him your confidence that since he began his good work in you, you are persuaded he will carry it on to completion. If this is a change in attitude for you (if you've been doubting or discouraged about his speed in completing his work in you), note how this change of heart impacts your circumstances.

WRAP UP
(5 minutes)

Next session, we'll explore the joy that comes from seeing God's Word advance into the secular culture. We'll hear Paul's joyful expression of watching God work through believers and even unbelievers to proclaim his truth and love to a world in desperate need of him. So, be on the lookout this week for opportunities to be a good witness to the truth about your faith in Christ.

Joyfully Exalting Christ

SESSION TWO

PHILIPPIANS 1:12–21

WELCOME and PRAYER
(5 minutes)

SHARE
(10 minutes)

Take turns sharing what you learned from applying the last session.

CONNECT
(15–20 minutes)

Back in the 1950s, Communism and its adherents went to extremes to squelch all mention of Christ, God, and the gospel from life behind the Iron Curtain. Christians were punished, imprisoned, or put to death. Bibles were forbidden and destroyed. School children were indoctrinated with lessons about the state and denied the opportunity to hear about the God of the Bible and how he intervened in human history in the person of Jesus Christ.

And yet, in the 1980s, as the curtain fell and the wall of Soviet Communism crumbled, the truth became obvious to the Western world that despite the persecution, devoted believers still lived in the former Soviet countries and served their master faithfully. The church of Jesus Christ, though battered and beaten, had survived.

Facilitator: Invite group members to participate in the following discussion.

It seems counterintuitive to think that when circumstances take trying or tragic turns for Christians, even then Christ is at work. And yet, it is a biblical truth. Share with the group the story of a time when you went through a challenge or difficulty you didn't understand only to find out later that God was at work in it to bring about your best interests.

DISCOVER
(10 minutes)

Complete the study notes as you watch the DVD together.

God wants us to experience _____, but how do we do this in the _____ of _____?

He writes, "I _____. And I will _____ to _____" (Phil. 1:18 NLT).

Paul had the right _____.

Philippians 1:12–21

Our problems are _____ the _____; it's how we choose to _____ at them.

The Praetorian guards were _____ personal _____—the most _____ people in all of Rome.

In a two-year span, Paul would witness to _____ of these guards.

If Paul would have seen his _____ as one big _____, he would have _____ God's great movement.

Paul had the right _____.

Paul writes, "So [long as] _____ is preached in every way possible, whether from _____ or _____ motives . . . I will continue to be _____" (Phil. 1:18 GNT).

When we make God our _____, everything, by nature, will _____ _____ accordingly.

Paul's third secret was _____.

_____ always outlasts our problems. Everything we face is temporal in light of eternity; that's _____.

> "To those who don't believe in God, life on earth is all there is, and so it is natural for them to strive for this world's values: money, popularity, power, pleasure, and prestige. For Paul, however, to live meant to develop eternal values and to tell others about Christ."
> —Life Application Study Bible

Finally, Paul had something to live for; he had _____.

There is so much _____ in our world today because there are so many people preoccupied with _____.

When you can say, "For me to _____ is _____," you will have more _____ than you could ever imagine.

DISCUSS
(25–30 minutes)

1. Speculate on why Paul began this section with, "Now I want you to know . . ." What was it that Paul wanted the people to know? Why was this so important for the believers to hear?

2. Since word had reached these friends that not only was Paul in chains, but that rivals were stirring up trouble for him, how might his reassurances in verses 13–18 have changed the Philippians' hearts and actions?

3. In today's post-Christian culture, what does it mean to put up a defense of the gospel? What might it cost? What might Paul tell us about speaking for Christ despite consequences?

Philippians 1:12–21

4. Consider words spoken by Joseph, another godly man held prisoner for doing right, "You intended to harm me, but God intended it for good to accomplish . . . the saving of many lives" (Gen. 50:20). Comment on the parallels between Joseph's words and Paul's words.

> The Greek words Paul uses tie the Philippians' prayers on his behalf with the help he received from Christ. This suggests that the help Christ provided was in response to the Philippians' prayers.

5. When have you seen Christ provide help to you in painful circumstances? How were prayers of fellow believers connected with the support you received from God?

6. Before reading verse 21, how would you have completed the statement, "For me, to live is . . ."? How does Paul's ending challenge you? What difference would it make if you really lived like Christ is your ultimate reward?

IMPLEMENT
(5–10 minutes)

Choose at least one activity to do before the next session. Tell one other person which item you chose.

1. Educate yourself about the persecuted Church. Pray daily for believers to be strengthened, to be bold in proclaiming Christ, and to be faithful to him.

2. Open your heart before God and ask him to reveal your motives for serving him. Are they from good will or selfish ambition? Make what he shows you a matter of fervent, continued prayer.

3. Be on the lookout for opportunities to advance the gospel. Be bold and speak out for Christ. Ask fellow believers to pray for you and hold you accountable.

WRAP UP
(5 minutes)

Read ahead to Philippians 2:1–5. Consider how your strained relationships with people on earth affect the joy you experience in Christ. Pray about this, and be ready to delve into it in next session.

Living in Joyful Relationship

PHILIPPIANS 2:1–5

SESSION THREE

WELCOME and PRAYER
(5 minutes)

SHARE
(10 minutes)

Take turns sharing what you learned from applying the last session.

CONNECT
(15–20 minutes)

She talked the Christian language at work and at church. She was always on the lookout for people with whom she could share Jesus Christ. She led prayer groups, volunteered for neighborhood witnessing, and donated large sums of money.

But what no one at work or church knew was that in her off hours, she frequented sordid places, where she was knowingly engaging in illegal acts. The thrill of the dual life energized her.

When it all unraveled and the truth came to light, instead of expressing shame, she said, "Now I can be his witness in the legal system." But unbelievers at her workplace and believers at church saw through that warped logic. The truth was, this vocal "believer" brought discredit to Christ whose name she brandished.

Facilitator: Invite group members to participate in the following discussion.

Leading into today's passage, Paul advises the Philippians, "Whatever happens, conduct yourselves in a manner worthy of the gospel of Christ" (Phil. 1:27). Take turns trying to describe what living worthy of the gospel looks like in everyday life. Why does it sometimes seem that unbelievers and skeptics know more about how Christians ought to conduct themselves than we do?

DISCOVER
(10 minutes)

Complete the study notes as you watch the DVD together.

Nothing robs our _____ more than _____.

Paul is simply saying, "If you really _____ this Jesus thing, here's what it will _____ _____."

Philippians 2:1–5

Two things can quickly rob our _____. The first is _____.

The moment we _____, we're no longer "_____-_____, having the same love, being one in _____ and _____" (Phil. 2:2).

The Bible says we are never to _____ anything that belongs to our _____. Why? It robs our _____.

Two things happen when we compare. First, we start _____ our responsibilities. Second, we start making _____ for every _____ we make.

Second, _____ robs our joy in relationship.

Conceit is "an _____ opinion of _____." Which means conceit is not just _____ oneself up, but also _____ oneself down. You're making _____ the center of attention; and that's _____.

Paul tells us how God's _____ are supposed to act in relationships: in _____.

> "When we work together, caring for the problems of others as if they were our problems, we demonstrate Christ's example of putting others first, and we experience unity. Don't be so concerned about making a good impression or meeting your own needs that you strain relationships in God's family."
> — Life Application Study Bible

> The Jamieson-Fausset-Brown Bible Commentary fleshes out Philippians 2:3 to read, "Instead of fixing your eyes on those points in which you excel, fix them on those in which your neighbor excels you: this is true 'humility.'"

Humility isn't thinking _____ of yourself; it is not _____ of yourself at all.

He brings us back to the great _____ _____: by faith, _____ Christ.

If we live like _____, the result will always be _____.

DISCUSS
(25–30 minutes)

1. In light of the suffering, Paul was undergoing and what he told the Philippians they ought to expect (1:29), what is the significance of his turning their immediate attention toward uniting their souls under the authority of God's Spirit?

2. List challenges we might encounter as we try to practice each element of the apostle's instructions in verse 2: becoming like-minded, maintaining love, uniting spirits, and pulling toward one objective. Why are these difficult for any body of Christ-followers to attain and maintain?

3. How might unity in love among the Philippians serve to increase Paul's joy and their own? How

Philippians 2:1–5

would their unity console him as he was chained to the guards? How would it prove them worthy of the gospel? How would it look to unbelievers?

4. Define the key terms introduced in verse 3: "selfish ambition," "vain conceit," and "humility." Compare and contrast these concepts, and give examples of what they look like in a church body.

> "Being of one accord— of one soul . . . The word used here does not occur elsewhere in the New Testament. It means a union of soul; or an acting together as if but one soul actuated them."
> —Albert Barnes

5. When you read, "Your attitude should be the same as that of Christ Jesus" (v. 5), what picture comes to your mind? Without reading further of Paul's description beginning in verse 6, how would you describe Jesus' attitude? How does it align with your attitude in your current circumstances? Where does it challenge you to repent and grow?

IMPLEMENT
(5–10 minutes)

Choose at least one activity to do before the next session. Tell one other person which item you chose.

1. Get alone before God and ask him to point out situations and relationships where you have put your own desires ahead of the best interests of

others. As he reveals these to you, commit that with the partnership of his Spirit, you will put on Christ's attitude and find ways to put that person or group's interests ahead of yours. Then act on what he places in your heart.

2. Since the *koinonia* (fellowship) of believers is crucial to the unity Paul describes, make time this week for fellowship with others from your Bible study group or church. As you spend this time together, actively listen with an open heart to what your fellow worshipers are saying—let them know by your actions that they are important to you.

WRAP UP
(5 minutes)

The Scripture for the next session (Phil. 2:6–11) is one of the most precious statements in the whole Bible. It paints the picture of what Christ willingly gave up to come to earth and see to our salvation. Meditate on Christ setting aside his rightful privileges and status as God to lower himself to our level and become one of us. Then express your awe and gratitude to him for this unfathomable sacrifice.

The King Becomes the Joyful Servant

SESSION FOUR

PHILIPPIANS 2:6–11

WELCOME and PRAYER
(5 minutes)

SHARE
(10 minutes)

Take turns sharing what you learned from applying the last session.

CONNECT
(15–20 minutes)

Mark Twain's 1881 classic story about a crown prince and a beggar exchanging places has fascinated young and old alike for generations. The pauper boy, Tom Canty, trades lives with Prince Edward, simply to see what the other's world is like.

While he is trying to escape from the abuses of Tom's beggar family, the rightful prince confronts injustices and class inequities he'd never encountered in his sheltered palace existence. He sees women abused.

The King Becomes the Joyful Servant

He sees people convicted and hanged on flimsy evidence for small-time crimes. And he is outraged. He promises that when he regains his place and rises to the throne he will reign in mercy—that just laws will mark his rule.

> "This is the foundational truth in Christianity. In this confession the early church affirmed the pre-existence of Jesus as God, affirmed His incarnation as a true human being, affirmed His death on the cross, His resurrection and His coming again to be revealed as Lord of all."
> —Lawrence O. Richards

Facilitator: Invite group members to participate in the following discussion.

Imagine what it would be like if a crown prince exchanged lives with you, if he lived in your household as one of your family. Which parts of your life would seem foreign, even humiliating, to someone raised as royalty—with expectations of one day assuming a country's ultimate authority? What if that Crown Prince was Jesus Christ, the Son of God, who will one day be crowned King of the Ages?

DISCOVER
(10 minutes)

Complete the study notes as you watch the DVD together.

Consistently, Jesus said, "_____ am _____."

Paul wrote, "Christ is the _____ image of the _____ God" (Col 1:15 paraphrase).

Philippians 2:6–11

The word *image* means _____, as in a photograph taken.

Paul continues: Jesus was _____. "He set aside the privilege of _____ and took on the status of a _____, became _____" (Phil. 2:7 MSG).

Why would God _____ to become one of _____?

For God to effectively communicate with us, he had to _____ us. The Bible calls this the _____.

He was _____ like us.

He _____ _____ like us.

He was _____ like us.

He _____ like us.

He became like us so we could _____ like _____.

Every other religion talks about who their _____ was; Christianity talks about who their leader _____ and _____ to come.

In the Greek, *Lord* means _____ or _____.

Christ is the only _____ in to heaven.

Is Jesus _____ of your life?

Paul wrote, "If you _____ with your mouth that Jesus is Lord and _____ in your heart that God raised him from the _____, you will be saved" (Rom. 10:9 ESV).

Every sphere of human _____ has been enriched by the name of _____.

DISCUSS
(25–30 minutes)

1. As you read about how Christ emptied himself to become what we are—bondservants and lowly humans—how do you feel about this condescension? Is there a part of you that bristles at the thought of your own lowliness? Why?

2. Commentator Adam Clarke asks, "What must sin have been in the sight of God, when it required such abasement in Jesus Christ to make an atonement for it?"* Consider this question, and discuss your answers.

3. Turn to Ephesians 1:20–23, and read this description of how high the Father has exalted Christ. How does this add to your understanding of how much Christ gave up for you? How does it affect your desire to worship him?

4. There will be two groups bowing to Christ in the last day: those who chose to acknowledge his lordship in this life, and those who chose to deny him. What is the difference between choosing to worship him and being forced to do so?

5. Reading Philippians 3:6–11 in context with verse 5 preceding them, how does Christ's obedient spirit and humility challenge you? Comment on what Paul's motivation might have been for placing this picture of Christ's sacrifice so near to his challenge to the believers to be unified in spirit under Christ's lordship.

> "The Incarnation was the act of the preexistent Son of God voluntarily assuming a human body and human nature. Without ceasing to be God, he became a human being, the man called Jesus. . . . He set aside the right to his glory and power."
> —Life Application Study Bible

IMPLEMENT
(5–10 minutes)

Choose at least one activity to do before the next session. Tell one other person which item you chose.

1. Memorize Philippians 2:10–11. To help, try envisioning the scene: the world's throngs, heavens' throngs, and the underworld's throngs gather. At one moment, every single knee bows to the Lord Christ. Picture the Father receiving glory from it.

2. This week as you're tempted to stand up for your rights, consider Christ who chose not to grasp for what was rightfully his, but became a humble, obedient servant. Ask for his grace to approach your situation with that same spirit.

3. Be sure that things are right between God and you. If you've never bowed your knee to confess Jesus Christ as your Lord and Savior, do it now—of your own volition and will. Ask for his forgiveness of your sin, and worship him for this gracious, unmerited gift he abased himself to give to you.

WRAP UP
(5 minutes)

In the next session, we'll unpack the truth about how spiritual change happens in our lives. We'll consider both how God changes us and our responsibility for our own growth toward him. Philippians 2:12–13 will help us get to the heart of who we are: our thoughts, our dependence on God, and the resources he has placed at our disposal.

NOTE

* Adam Clarke, *A Commentary and Critical Notes* (New York: Abingdon-Cokesbury Press, 1826), http://www.studylight.org/com/acc/view.cgi?book=php&chapter=002 (accessed March 10, 2010).

God's Work, the Believer's Work

SESSION FIVE

PHILIPPIANS 2:12–13

WELCOME and PRAYER
(5 minutes)

SHARE
(10 minutes)

Take turns sharing what you learned from applying the last session.

CONNECT
(15–20 minutes)

"No touch," the mom tells her toddler as she points to the fiery burner. "Hot!"

"Hot!" the baby parrots. Then, as she holds her mother's eye, she reaches a plump little hand and touches the spot her mother told her to avoid. It's not that she doesn't understand her mother's command; it's that she wants to find out for herself how bad "hot" could really be.

Never mind that mommy has always protected her lovingly; there is something inside that motivates her to defiance and disobedience.

Then come the consequences. "Ouch!" She cries and wails until mommy offers first aid and kisses it to make it better. Will it be a lesson learned, or will her defiance show up again later?

Facilitator: Invite group members to participate in the following discussion.

What is it about the word *obedience* that makes our independent natures squirm? Share with the group a time when you balked at obeying something you were asked to do, something you knew would be best for you. Talk about why you disobeyed and what consequences you suffered as a result. Tell whether you'd change your actions now if you could.

DISCOVER
(10 minutes)

Complete the study notes as you watch the DVD together.

Paul writes, "Continue to _____ _____ your salvation with _____ and _____" (Phil. 2:12 TNIV).

The first tool God uses is _____.

Philippians 2:12–13

If we're serious about change, the _____ is required reading.

The more we get into the _____, the more the _____ will come out in our lives.

The second tool God uses to work in our salvation is the _____ _____.

> "Paul now turns to the obligations that the example of Christ lays on the Philippian Christians. They must learn to stand on their own feet, with a sense of human frailty but knowing that God was behind them."
> —Charles Ryrie

Paul tells us that we are not to be controlled by the _____ _____, but in the spirit of Christ—the Spirit that _____ within us.

It is in God's _____ that we find the _____ to change.

The third tool God uses to work in our salvation is our _____.

The Bible says, "In everything _____ works for the _____ of those who _____ him" (Rom. 8:28 NCV).

God is more interested in our _____ than he is our _____.

So then, what is our _____?

First, we have to carefully _____ what we think about.

If we want to make godly changes, it starts with our _____.

> *The fact of Paul's absence from his beloved Philippian church is significant to his direction for them to work out their salvation. It stems from his desire to see the Philippians depend not on his guidance, but on their individual, personal relationships with Christ for direction according to the Father's will.*

Second, we have to _____ to be _____ to God's Spirit.

It is imperative that we be _____ to the Spirit's _____.

Finally, we have to _____ how we will _____ in all situations.

God uses our _____; we get to choose how we will _____ in them.

DISCUSS
(25–30 minutes)

1. Paul introduces this dicey directive (*obey*) by calling his readers, "my beloved" (NASB). What difference do you suppose it made to the original hearers that Paul wasn't making a demand out of jealousy, selfishness, or obstinacy, but rather

Philippians 2:12–13

out of a loving desire to see them receive God's best benefits? How does this affect your reading?

2. According to verse 12, motivation plays into our choice to do right or wrong. Are we choosing right because someone is watching, or will we do it even if no one seems to take notice? What difference does it make?

3. Consider possible reasons Paul chose to include the phrase, "with fear and trembling." What does this rather unsettling word picture add to your understanding of how important this directive is to the true believer? What kind of fear do you suppose the apostle means for us to have? What ought this fear lead us to do?

> *Whenever true believers find themselves not feeling like doing God's will, even then they can find the strength to do right. It is found in the Spirit of God at work within the believer's heart, not only pointing out the Father's will, but apportioning the will to do it.*

4. Grapple with the balance between working out what we believe and trusting God to work in us. Discuss the illustration of breathing out and breathing in. How does this help you process verses 12–13?

5. What is our responsibility in finding and doing God's good purpose? What does he offer to do on our behalf? How can we tap into his work in us?

IMPLEMENT
(5–10 minutes)

Choose at least one activity to do before the next session. Tell one other person which item you chose.

In response to the resources God has placed in your hands, commit this week to:

1. Read his Word every day, even if only a few verses. Meditate on what you read.

2. Pray that his Spirit will enlighten your eyes to understand how his word is relevant to your life that day, and that he will equip you to act accordingly.

3. Watch for God's clear leading as the circumstances of your week unfold. Ask for his wisdom to recognize what he is doing in your life. And then get on board with him.

WRAP UP
(5 minutes)

Next session we'll see how complaining and arguing has a negative impact on the way we demonstrate Christ's love to a watching world. Seek God's strength and motivation to behave in a way that would honor rather than displease him.

Joyfully Blameless, Living among Scoffers

SESSION SIX

PHILIPPIANS 2:14–15

WELCOME and PRAYER
(5 minutes)

SHARE
(10 minutes)

Take turns sharing what you learned from applying the last session.

CONNECT
(15–20 minutes)

Imagine being a chaperone about to embark on a three-thousand-mile ministry tour with two dozen sleep-deprived people, teenagers from your church youth group with raging hormones and feisty personalities staying in close quarters for two weeks.

If you were preparing for that trip (you'd only do it once in a lifetime), what Scripture would you ask everyone to memorize as your tour theme?

Maybe not John 3:16 or anything in Romans. Here's the verse that might serve your sanity best: "Do everything without complaining or arguing" (Phil. 2:14). If the group could pull that off, maybe it would be a great ministry trip.

Facilitator: Invite group members to participate in the following discussion.

> The imagery of a light shining is one Jesus used in Matthew 5:14–16. Neither in Jesus' usage nor in Paul's was it meant to be our own lights shining. Rather, it is in our reflecting the light of the majestic glory of Christ that we hold out for others the life-giving truth of the gospel.

Have two volunteers pick a silly argument with each other. It can be about rival sports teams or favorite colors or a book they've read. Give them two minutes to disagree loudly. While they're arguing, try to have a quiet conversation within the rest of the group.

Once you call time, talk about how hard it was to have a quiet conversation in the midst of bickering.

DISCOVER
(10 minutes)

Complete the study notes as you watch the DVD together.

Paul says, "Do everything without _____ or _____, so that you may become _____ and _____, children of God without fault in a crooked and depraved generation" (Phil 2:14–15).

Philippians 2:14–15

There are three "to dos" when it comes to _____ complaining.

First, don't _____, but _____.

Complaining is not just a _____ habit, it's _____, and _____ has consequences.

> "Are you shining brightly, or are you clouded by complaining and arguing? Don't let dissensions snuff out your light. Shine out for God. Your role is to shine until Jesus returns and bathes the world in his radiant glory."
> —Life Application Study Bible

Second, don't be _____, but _____. Rather, be _____ to each other and to _____ else.

The Scripture doesn't say we are to be _____ *for* all circumstances, but rather, we are to be _____ *in* all circumstances. Why? Because God's _____ for our life is always _____ than any problems.

Paul tells us to "Let the _____ that comes from Christ to control our _____ and be grateful" (Col. 3:15 CEV).

Finally, don't _____, _____.

Instead of being _____, be _____. Use words that build someone _____, instead of beat them _____.

"Speak _____ words to one another. Build up _____" (1 Thess. 5:11 MSG).

Affirmation always gets _____ results than _____ and/or complaining.

DISCUSS
(25–30 minutes)

1. Consider and comment on the parallel construction of Paul's instructions in verses 14–15: *Don't* grumble or dispute; *do* be blameless and innocent. Others translate the *do* section as "be harmless and sincere." How do grumbling, disputing, and complaining affect our pure standing before God? How do they affect how outsiders view both Christ and Christianity?

2. Mull over two concepts that are introduced here in Philippians and are fleshed out in greater detail in Ephesians 5:1–7: the great privilege of being called "dearly loved children" of the living God; and the awesome responsibility of carrying that name.

3. Paint a word picture of what Philippians 2:15 calls being "without fault" (NIV) or "above reproach" (NASB) looks like in everyday life. Return to Ephesians 5, and discuss what a crooked and depraved

Philippians 2:14–15

lifestyle looks like. How do these two divergent pictures challenge you to make specific lifestyle changes?

4. The concept of believers shining like stars in the heavens continues into Philippians 2:16 by tying into holding out the word of life. Commentators suggest the allusion is to lighthouses that marked harbor openings for seafarers. How can believers provide that kind of light to spiritual seafarers seeking safe harbor in Christ?

> Albert Barnes notes that Christians will always be living "among those of perverted sentiments and habits; those who are disposed to complain and find fault; those who will take every occasion to pervert what you do and say, and who seek every opportunity to retard the cause of truth and righteousness."

IMPLEMENT
(5–10 minutes)

Choose at least one activity to do before the next session. Tell one other person which item you chose.

1. Take seriously Paul's challenge to do everything "without complaining or arguing." Make every effort to avoid arrogant disagreements within the body of believers. Where you and another believer disagree, actively pursue ways to respect each other in love.

2. What personal habits or besetting sins came to mind as you read the lesson? Consider these to be conviction from God's Spirit. Seek his forgiveness for these sins and his strength to repent—to turn away from them and stop sinning.

3. This week you will certainly encounter dark enclaves in your world, places where the light of Christ is sorely needed. Now that you are clean and blameless before him, ask for the privilege of reflecting his light in those places. Look for ways to hold out the life-giving word to people caught in darkness.

WRAP UP
(5 minutes)

Next session we'll discover the keys to living a consistent Christian life so you can enjoy the benefits of a lifetime of faith. To prepare your heart and mind for the study, take time on your own to read Philippians 3:1–10. Focus, especially on verse 10, considering how much it means to you to know God in personal relationship through Jesus Christ your Lord.

Joy in Loss and Loss in Gain

SESSION SEVEN

PHILIPPIANS 3:1–10

WELCOME and PRAYER
(5 minutes)

SHARE
(10 minutes)

Take turns sharing what you learned from applying the last session.

CONNECT
(15–20 minutes)

A song made the rounds of contemporary Christian music a decade or so ago. It told the story of a man who hit midlife and decided to toss away his marriage for an illicit affair, trade in his faith for a life of license to sin, and forego his commitments to pursue immediate pleasure. Essentially, he was living the life of soap operas and Hollywood movies.

The songwriter asked a question about this man, and perhaps about our own choices: What if he woke up to find himself gasping beneath the deepest depths, rather than soaring above the highest mountain. Or, to put it another way, what if he awoke to find that he was living life upside down?

Facilitator: Invite group members to participate in the following discussion.

This idea of biblical values being upside down when compared to our culture's values is worth considering. Together, list at least a dozen specific ways our culture's value system is exactly opposite of God's life-plan for his people. Take note of the insidious ways culture communicates its values—gets them under our skin and entices us to accept them without examination.

DISCOVER
(10 minutes)

Complete the study notes as you watch the DVD together.

Paul gives three _____ on how to maintain our _____.

First, Paul tells us to live by _____, not by _____, which substitutes rules for _____.

Jesus confronted the Pharisees about legalism: "You load people down with _____ and

Philippians 3:1–10

"_____, nearly breaking their backs" (Luke 11:46 MSG).

"You cannot make _____ accept you because of _____ you _____" (Rom. 4:5 CEV).

"For it is by _____ we have been saved, through _____ — this is not from yourselves, it is a gift from _____" (Eph. 2:8 TNIV).

_____ and _____ will always be enemies.

> To a generation that watched financial markets swing from gains to losses (sometimes within the same day), Paul's use of these terms has clear implications. Paul's fortunes against human measures swung from gain to loss when he entrusted himself to Christ. But his fortunes in light of eternity swung from bankrupt to immeasurable wealth in the same transaction.

Second, we need to let go of the _____ in our life.

"I once thought these things were valuable, but now I consider them _____ because of what _____ has done" (Phil. 3:7 NLT).

Third, _____ to _____ God.

"All I _____ is to _____ Christ" (Phil. 3:10 GNT).

The word *know* in Greek means to know _____.

DISCUSS
(25–30 minutes)

1. What personal achievements or spiritual milestones are you most proud to call your own? About what are you most tempted to boast, either aloud or in your heart?

2. Why does Paul consider his best accomplishments a loss? What temptations might boasting about these accomplishments place in a believer's path?

> Regarding Paul's phrase, "And be found in him," Albert Barnes comments, "The idea is, that when the investigations of the great day should take place in regard to the ground of salvation, it might be found that he was united to the Redeemer, and depended solely on his merits for salvation."

3. How did Christ respond during his earthly ministry to those who claimed his father's name but trusted in their own accomplishments (for example, the religious leaders)?

4. If you're holding onto your own merits, how difficult is it to take hold of Christ? Why?

5. How did you (or can you) come to the place Paul described where you can honestly count all your treasured accomplishments "rubbish" or "dung" in comparison to knowing your Savior? Describe the joy you find in this unlikely exchange.

Philippians 3:1–10

6. Twice in the passage Paul refers to a driving desire to know Christ. What kind of knowing do you suppose Paul meant? Read Ephesians 2:7–20, and discuss what you discover there about how Paul described knowing Christ.

> There is a passion and intensity in Paul's cry, "That I may know Him" (Phil. 3:10 NASB). Not surface knowledge. Not knowing about him from a distance. But knowing him, in his glory, his righteousness, his power—and even (or perhaps especially) his suffering.

7. Paul used both positive terms (righteousness, faith, power, fellowship, and resurrection) and negative terms (sufferings and death) regarding his desire to be found in Christ. What can suffering and death add to our joy in relationship with Christ?

IMPLEMENT
(5–10 minutes)

Choose at least one activity to do before the next session. Tell one other person which item you chose.

1. Like Paul did in verses 4–6, make a list of all of your spiritual accomplishments, everything you have to offer to Christ. Then, write in big letters across the list, R-U-B-B-I-S-H. In prayer, offer yourself to him not based on your merits, but exclusively trusting his grace.

2. If your true heart's passion is to know Christ, spend part of your quiet hour each day reading the Gospels. Pay special attention to the moments when Jesus opens the curtain of heaven and describes what his father is like. Take note of his interactions with individual sufferers and seekers. Experience his passion for you through his prayers on your behalf and his death for your sins. Ask that his Spirit will reveal him to you—personally, up-close, more and more each day.

WRAP UP
(5 minutes)

Perfectionists among us, listen up, and those who know they can't possibly measure up, take heart: Next session will be all about the fact that the pursuit of Christ's high calling on our lives is a race, a journey, a process in Philippians 3:12–14. We haven't arrived yet, but we can be more into the journey if we divest ourselves of things that are holding us back and commit to moving forward.

Joy in Running to Win

PHILIPPIANS 3:12–14

SESSION EIGHT

WELCOME and PRAYER
(5 minutes)

SHARE
(10 minutes)

Take turns sharing what you learned from applying the last session.

CONNECT
(15–20 minutes)

Competition. We thrive on it, whether college bowl games, last-one-standing reality shows, or super-chef challenges. When we compete, someone has to win and someone has to lose.

Marshall Shelley, editor of *Leadership Journal,* asks, "What is it about us that obsesses on identifying winners? I'm reminded of the story about a Raj from India who, while visiting America, declined an invitation to attend a derby, explaining, 'The fact that one horse can run faster than others is both obvious and trivial.'"*

Yet there is one element of competition that is worthwhile to all involved—that of doing our best, pressing ourselves beyond human limits to achieve something worthwhile, such as a goal, a prize, or a sense of triumph.

Facilitator: Invite group members to participate in the following discussion.

Describe your experiences as the winner in some discipline and the loser in the same or another discipline—sports, academics, workplace achievements, or even weight-loss achievements (where winners are losers). Where have you come out ahead of or behind others? How did you feel as a winner? As a loser? Did you do your best or coast? How did that affect your feelings about the competition—whether you won or lost?

DISCOVER
(10 minutes)

Complete the study notes as you watch the DVD together.

The first key [to success] is a willingness to _____ our _____.

Philippians 3:12–14

"I do not claim that I have already _____ or have already become _____" (Phil. 3:12 GNT).

Once you take that needless pressure for _____ off yourself, you can start to work on those areas that need little _____.

Successful people _____ _____ growing. They're always _____.

The second key is to _____ the past. Success means learning to _____ _____.

Whatever was, no longer is, so quit _____ on it.

The third key to success is to _____ your life.

> *We can take courage in the knowledge that at this late stage of Paul's journey with Christ, he still didn't consider he had yet taken hold of everything he pursued. The word we translate as perfect, in the Greek means "to bring to an end, to complete." If Paul wouldn't be there until he'd breathed his last, there is yet hope for us.*

"Concentrate on _____ your _____ for God" (2 Tim. 2:15 MSG).

Paul says, "I have my _____ clearly in mind" (Phil. 3:14 paraphrase).

There is tremendous power when we are _____ and _____.

Joy in Running to Win

Paul's final key is to _____ a good _____.

Press on in Greek means, "I _____ for ____ with _____ I've got."

> Anne Ortlund writes, "We're little amateur psychologists these days . . . to explain all our idiosyncrasies and quirks. The Bible doesn't so deal with us. It pronounces us sinners and then says to get on with it, to look up and forward!"

"Give it _____ you have, _____ and soul" (Josh. 1:7 MSG).

God gave us his _____; we are obligated to _____ him ours.

DISCUSS
(25–30 minutes)

1. At this stage of the apostle's life, what spiritual blessings has he already obtained from Christ? What promises has God fulfilled for him? What was he still waiting for or pressing toward? Now answer each of those questions from your life.

2. Revisit your notes from last lesson. How do the keys of fully knowing Christ and being found in him relate to the "all this" that Paul has yet to obtain?

3. The phrase, "that for which Christ Jesus took hold of me" (v. 12), indicates Christ has a purpose for your life that is not yet completed. Discuss what this

Philippians 3:12–14

purpose might be and your feelings about continuing toward this goal.

4. How can glancing back at things in your past, whether reliving glowing moments or wallowing in sins now forgiven, derail you spiritually?

5. Consider the image of a believer straining toward a goal, putting every last gasp of effort into it as if it were the last one hundred feet of a marathon, with your body fighting your will at every footfall. When has your journey with Christ felt that way? How did you find the strength to press on? What encouragement can you offer to a believer who might be feeling that strain today?

> "Forgetting what lies behind. *The past accomplishments of his Christian career, which might induce self-satisfaction and a slackening of pace.* Straining forward *graphically portrays a runner who draws upon all his remaining strength and stretches out toward the goal (thus, our homestretch)."*
> —The Wycliffe Bible Commentary

IMPLEMENT
(5–10 minutes)

Choose at least one activity to do before the next session. Tell one other person which item you chose.

1. Compare your efforts this week on home- or work-related goals to your effort and energy pursuing the

knowledge of Christ. Bring what you discover before the Lord in prayer.

2. Prayerfully list all the things behind you that are weighing down your race toward the finish line with Christ. Let God know you are putting off each one of these things. Then get rid of them so you can move forward with him.

3. Read the apostle John's glowing description of the future that awaits believers in Revelation 22. Consider this the prize you are running toward, and find in its promise the strength to press on.

WRAP UP
(5 minutes)

Next session, we'll skip ahead to Philippians 4:6–8 where we'll learn Paul's prescription for our anxiety malady. Meditate during the week on Philippians 3:14—4:5.

NOTE

* Marshall Shelley, e-mail to Leadership Weekly mailing list, January 12, 2010.

Joy Encircled in God's Protection

PHILIPPIANS 4:6-8

SESSION NINE

WELCOME and PRAYER
(5 minutes)

SHARE
(10 minutes)

Take turns sharing what you learned from applying the last session.

CONNECT
(15–20 minutes)

They returned from their honeymoon to a house payment, two car payments, and credit cards maxed out from the wedding and the trip. If they got the raises they expected, they could just make ends meet. But, what if . . . ?

Then financial markets plummeted. Their house was worth less than they owed on it. The husband lost his job. The wife's company went into austerity—with wages frozen and days without pay.

Yet, they weathered the storm. Somehow, God provided. They didn't starve. They still had a roof over their heads.

One thought continually gnawed at their minds: *What good did all those sleepless nights do to change our circumstances?*

Facilitator: Invite group members to participate in the following discussion.

Identify and share about a time when you worried about something you thought might happen. If it did happen, how much did your energy invested in worry change the situation? If it didn't ever happen, how much energy did you squander worrying about it? What do you wish you had done with that energy instead?

DISCOVER
(10 minutes)

Complete the study notes as you watch the DVD together.

Paul writes, "Don't _____ about _____" (Phil. 4:6 GNT).

Paul gives three keys for _____ worry.

First, _____ about _____.

Philippians 4:6–8

When we worry, we're not _____ God; we're _____ ourselves.

"Each day that we live, he will _____ for our _____" (Ps. 103:5 CEV).

Paul's second key is to be _____ in _____ things.

"_____ _____ in all circumstances, for this is God's _____ for you in Christ Jesus" (1 Thess. 5:18).

Paul's third key is to _____ _____ the right things.

Sow a _____, reap an _____. Sow an _____, reap a _____. Sow a _____, reap a _____.

Worry is not an _____ situation, it's an _____ disposition.

> "The words 'be anxious' (merimnao, 4:6) can refer to being unduly concerned about anything, but it is often used in contexts where persecution is the issue. Thus both Matthew and Luke use this word in their record of Jesus' admonition to his disciples not to be concerned about what they will say before the local councils, governors, and kings who hunt them down."
> —*NIV Application Commentary, New Testament*

"Blessed are those who _____ in the LORD and have made the LORD their _____ and _____" (Jer. 17:7 NLT).

Joy Encircled in God's Protection

> Adam Clarke makes this jarring observation about Philippians 4:6–7: "God alone can help you; he is disposed to do it, but you must ask by prayer and supplication; without this he has not promised to help you."

Choose to _____, be _____, and _____ about the right things, and the cares of this world will _____.

DISCUSS
(25–30 minutes)

1. Why do you suppose anxiety is such a perennially successful weapon that Satan uses against believers? When we worry, what are we saying about our faith in God's promises?

2. Paul isn't the only one to challenge us to stop worrying. Jesus makes a similar challenge in Luke 12:22–32. Read that passage and discuss what Jesus says about seeking his kingdom first. How does that affect our propensity to worry?

3. Prayer, supplication, and thanksgiving are part of Paul's prescription. How does this build on Jesus' instruction? How do these work together to assuage a heart in the grip of panic?

4. Paul offers God's peace when we exchange anxiety for thankful prayer. Why peace? Why not love or

Philippians 4:6–8

mercy or compassion? What is it about God's peace that is the perfect guard for the anxious heart?

5. How does what we allow our minds to dwell on affect our physical health? Our spiritual health? Why is it important to protect our minds from dwelling on things that are opposite to pure, true, right, lovely, or praiseworthy? What ways have you found to guard your mind from evil? In what ways does Philippians 4:8 remain a challenge for you?

> *Guard in verse 7 is a military term that means "a watcher in advance," "a sentinel," or to "hem in, protect: keep (with a garrison)," according to Strong's Greek Dictionary. The word picture is of God's garrison of peace as our encircling guard.*

IMPLEMENT
(5–10 minutes)

Choose at least one activity to do before the next session. Tell one other person which item you chose.

1. At regular intervals one weekday (perhaps once every half hour), stop what you're doing and jot a quick note about what you were thinking. Before you go to sleep, review the day's list. Pray about each item, especially those that caused you distress. Picture God encircling you with his garrison of peace. Then lie down to rest

peacefully, being convinced that God's mounted guard of protection is sufficient.

2. Take to heart Paul's challenge to think about things that are pure, honorable, true, lovely, etc. One place to find such good things is in the word of God. Each morning as you are having coffee or eating breakfast, put a promise of God into your mind. One good place to start is Jesus' Sermon on the Mount (Matt. 5–7).

WRAP UP
(5 minutes)

Contentment is a key ingredient of biblical, lasting joy. Yet it is in short supply in an instant-gratification culture. Paul learned the secret of contentment, and he eagerly shared it with his beloved Philippian believers. Next session, you'll dig into Philippians 4:11–13 and find that secret to be true for your life challenges, as well.

Joyfully Satisfied in Christ

LESSON TEN

PHILIPPIANS 4:11–13

WELCOME and PRAYER
(5 minutes)

SHARE
(10 minutes)

Take turns sharing what you learned from applying the last session.

CONNECT
(15–20 minutes)

"I'm satisfied with just a cottage below a little silver and a little gold."

So begins an old gospel song titled "Mansion Over the Hilltop." The song's narrator finds the ability to be satisfied with rags and rubble here on earth, because he's looking toward the sparkling, new, eternal home promised to every believer in Revelation 21. The place where there is no sin, no death, and no sorrow. The place where mansions are glistening, city streets are paved with purest gold, and walls are laden with gemstones of every color and description.

Temporary shack versus eternal palace. Sure, he can endure the lack here in the moment, because he's looking toward a future of eternal abundance. Not a bad tradeoff, actually.

Facilitator: Invite group members to participate in the following discussion.

Discuss what it takes for a person in today's post-modern culture to be satisfied. How does the entire culture seem to conspire to keep us dissatisfied—keep us wanting the next product, the next great advancement, the next thrill that will take us swifter, higher, and longer than we've ever been before? What is the danger to us if we buy into that mindset? How can we keep from falling into culture's trap?

DISCOVER
(10 minutes)

Complete the study notes as you watch the DVD together.

We can live a life of _____. The secret? Paul writes, "I have _____ to be content whatever the _____" (Phil. 4:11).

The first lesson is that we learn to _____ ourselves.

Philippians 4:11–13

"Don't _____ yourself with _____" (Gal. 6:4 MSG).

Ephesians 2:10 reads, "We are God's _____" (NLT).

God paid the highest _____ of all—his very own _____ for you.

Paul says, "I don't give my time to comparing myself to _____; I give my time to keeping my eyes on _____."

> "Content: The Greek, literally expresses 'independent of others, and having sufficiency in one's self.' But Christianity has raised the term above the haughty self-sufficiency of the heathen Stoic to the contentment of the Christian, whose sufficiency is not in self, but in God."
> —Jamieson-Fausset-Brown Bible Commentary

Second, if we're going to learn to be _____, we have to _____ our circumstances.

The word *content* means _____-_____. But when Paul uses it, he means his _____-_____ resource is in the Lord.

Epictetus wrote, "I know that what God _____ is better than what I would _____."

Paul knew the Lord would never _____ no matter what he _____.

Despite what is happening _____ us, our focus should be what is happening _____ us.

Joyfully Satisfied in Christ

> Adam Clarke wrote out that Paul "was thoroughly instructed; fully initiated into all the mysteries of poverty and want, and of the supporting hand of God in the whole. See here the state to which God permitted his chief apostle to be reduced! And see how powerfully the grace of Christ supported him under the whole!"

Paul's final key in learning to live a life of contentment is to accept a _____ and _____ his will for our lives.

Paul is saying, "Jesus Christ is the _____ of my life. He gives me continuous _____. I never run out."

DISCUSS
(25–30 minutes)

1. How would you express a personal definition of *contentment* in your lifestyle and circumstances? How often would you honestly describe yourself as content? What challenges or unsettles your spiritual contentment?

2. What is the difference between being self-satisfied and being satisfied in Christ? In which of these states will you find true contentment? Support your answer with other Scriptures that you can recall.

3. Paul's secret for contentment is found in verse 13, which translates in essence to the all-sufficient generosity of God through Jesus Christ. When in your life have you seen God strengthen and equip

Philippians 4:11–13

you to do what you would have considered impossible? How does recounting this situation build up your faith? How does it affect your feeling of contentment in your current circumstances?

4. Consider Paul's statement in Galatians 2:20 that Christ, who lives in him, is the source of the life he now lives by faith. How is that consistent with Philippians 4:13?

> "Paul's own understanding of 'need' (vv. 11–13) is the key to understanding the term here, . . . God will supply the Philippians with . . . the ability to face all circumstances through the one who gives them strength (v. 13)."
> —Frank Thielman

5. How do these potent statements about Paul's dependence on God's strength challenge you? What have you been trying to do in your own strength? What tasks that face you obviously require God's strength to accomplish? How will you tap into that strength? What do you think Christ would tell you to do about this need?

IMPLEMENT
(5–10 minutes)

Choose at least one activity to do before the next session. Tell one other person which item you chose.

1. One of the apostle's challenges was to live within humble means. Take up the challenge this week

by cutting out one luxury or personal splurge item in your budget. Do it willingly, not grudgingly. Use the extra resources to do something for someone else or for the betterment of God's kingdom. Consider how this experiment affects your level of contentment.

2. Earlier, Paul challenged believers to put aside grumbling or complaining. Now he challenges us to be content. Journal about how these concepts are connected. Prayerfully make notes about times in the past week when you have been lacking in contentment and tempted to express that emotion by complaining. Confess those times before the Lord and ask for his strength to overcome them.

WRAP UP
(5 minutes)

The Philippians' generosity of spirit was a joy to the apostle Paul and could become a source of joy to the givers, as well. This will be the focus of next session's study of Philippians 4:14–18. Read ahead as you prepare your heart. Then listen for the Spirit's prompting regarding the abundance he has provided you and his desire for you to be willing to share it with others.

The Joy of Sharing Generously

SESSION ELEVEN

PHILIPPIANS 4:14–18

WELCOME and PRAYER
(5 minutes)

SHARE
(10 minutes)

Take turns sharing what you learned from applying the last session.

CONNECT
(15–20 minutes)

Say the word *miserly* and you conjure the picture of old Ebenezer Scrooge. Charles Dickens introduced him as "a squeezing, wrenching, grasping, scraping, clutching, covetous, old sinner!" Such is the spirit of one who hoards wealth.

But, as generations of readers will recall, that wasn't the end of Scrooge. After a single night spent cold-faced against the frightening reality of the end saved for such misers, he took it upon himself to evoke such

The Joy of Sharing Generously

a change that he became the opposite of his old self—a joyful, generous giver.

Whether this drastic change can take place by mere human effort is questionable. But for one who believes in Christ and becomes generous because of him, it is not only possible but guaranteed.

> "What makes money so magnetic and giving it away so stressful? Money measures our energy; it represents our day-to-day security. Giving money away puts our work and our futures at risk. . . . once you've determined that a project honors the Lord, don't hold back—give generously and joyfully. Like the Philippians, you'll be establishing an eternal partnership."
> —Life Application Study Bible

Facilitator: Invite group members to participate in the following discussion.

Tell of a time when you have been the recipient of someone else's generosity. How did you feel as you received the needed gift that kept you afloat in a difficult time? Now, tell of a time when you have been the giver to someone in true need. What was your motivation for giving? What effect did the act of giving have on you?

DISCOVER
(10 minutes)

Complete the study notes as you watch the DVD together.

The key to joy-filled living is found in _____-_____ _____.

Philippians 4:14–18

"A generous man will _____; he who refreshes others will himself be _____" (Prov. 11:25).

Paul gives three reasons to be _____. First, it _____ the receiver.

The word *encouragement* means to _____ with courage and _____.

Second, Paul tells us that _____ is an _____ investment.

Every _____ given is _____ and rewarded.

Paul says, "Be _____ in good works and give _____ to those in need; always being ready to _____ with others whatever God has given them" (1 Tim. 6:18 NLT).

"It is a good work to succour and help a good minister in trouble. The nature of true Christian sympathy, is not only to feel concern for our friends in their troubles, but to do what we can to help them."
—Matthew Henry

Finally, generosity is _____ by God. God is _____ when we give.

We are most like _____ when we are _____.

Jesus said, "It is more _____ to give than to _____" (Acts 20:35 NLT).

We must first be _____ to others.

DISCUSS
(25–30 minutes)

1. How was the sacrificial gift the Philippians sent a source of Paul's gratitude and contentment? What joy might they have found in helping meet the apostle's physical needs? How was their gift part of God's answering their prayers for the apostle?

2. In Mark 12:41–44, Jesus talks about the spirit of the giver. How does this color your reading of Paul's comments about the gift he received from the Philippians?

3. Paul seems sad when he points out that only this church, and none other, participated with him in the advance of the gospel. Why is partnership with other believers so critical to someone on the front lines of ministry? For hints, notice the desperate loneliness in the prophet Elijah's voice in 1 Kings 19:14. How does the knowledge of others being with them in spirit bolster both Paul (Phil. 1:7) and Elijah (1 Kings 19:18)? What implications does this have for your interaction with those on the front lines of ministry?

> "[T]he odour of a sweet smell . . . *is drawn from the sweet-smelling incense which was burnt along with the sacrifices; their gift being in faith was not so much to Paul, as to God.*"
> —Jamieson-Fausset-Brown Bible Commentary

Philippians 4:14–18

4. In Romans 12:1, Paul mentions another kind of sacrifice that is pleasing to God. Compare and contrast the two different sacrifices (financial and spiritual). Then read what Jesus said in John 4:23–24. Put the pieces together from these three passages to compose a more complete understanding of how God perceives our gifts.

IMPLEMENT
(5–10 minutes)

Choose at least one activity to do before the next session. Tell one other person which item you chose.

1. Survey your resources—finances, talents, possessions, and anything else of value you could offer to God. Seek his direction on what he might have you give away for the work of the gospel. Before you give, do research on the ministries you will support. This will help you determine where finances can be used most effectively and equip you to pray intelligently as a spiritual partner with the minister.

2. Write an e-mail, card, or letter to your pastor or to a missionary your church supports. Include a small gift and express appreciation for the ways this person represents Christ and works for him.

Assure this minister of the gospel that you are standing together with him or her in prayer.

WRAP UP
(5 minutes)

Next session we'll focus on just one verse: Philippians 4:19. It's a crucial one, though, and worthy of in-depth study. As the Philippians were willing to do everything possible to supply the apostle's need, God would do more than they could ever imagine to meet their deepest needs. Prayerfully consider the implications that fact has for your life as you prepare to wrap up this study.

Joy in God's Rich Supply

PHILIPPIANS 4:19

SESSION TWELVE

WELCOME and PRAYER
(5 minutes)

SHARE
(10 minutes)

Take turns sharing what you learned from applying the last session.

CONNECT
(15–20 minutes)

"But Mom, I *need* that new pair of athletic shoes. I'll be the team joke if I show up in last year's raggedy shoes. Anyway, my toes are practically coming through the old ones. See? They're wearing thin. Come on. Don't you love me? You wouldn't want the guys pushing me around. And all for a measly pair of shoes. You could afford them. My birthday's coming up in a few months. Give them to me now, and give me less then. I'll never ask you for anything ever again."

We can laugh at that uniquely teen-aged monologue. Yet, how many times do we enter God's presence begging for something we *need* in just those terms?

Facilitator: Invite group members to participate in the following discussion.

Tell the story of a time when you begged for something you just had to have—it could be something you begged from your parent, your spouse, or even from God. What was the result of your begging? If you received the gift, was it everything you anticipated? If you didn't receive it, how did you handle it? Looking back, was it a need or a want? How do you know that?

DISCOVER
(10 minutes)

Complete the study notes as you watch the DVD together.

Solomon wrote, "Be _____, and _____ you will be rewarded" (Eccl. 11:1 CEV).

Now, let's look at the _____ of God in response to being _____.

"And my God will meet _____ your _____, according to his glorious _____ in Christ Jesus" (Phil. 4:19).

Philippians 4:19

First, Paul says he's _____ _____. For the promise to become _____, it has to become _____.

Jesus said, "A person is a _____ to store up earthly _____ but not have a rich _____ with _____" (Luke 12:21 NLT).

We must come to a place in our hearts, as Paul said, "All I want is to _____ is _____" (Phil. 3:10 CEV).

The second part of the promise says, he will _____ all our _____.

Peter wrote, "[As we know _____ better,] his _____ _____ . . . give[s] us _____ we need" (2 Pet. 1:3 NLT).

Merrill Unger describes glory as the "distinctive excellence" of God, or the "manifestation of His divine attributes and perfections." Unger explains God's glory is the embodiment of his holiness. Out of that holy glory flows provision sufficient for our need.

The third part of the promise says, "according to his _____ _____ in Christ Jesus" (Phil. 4:19).

According to means *in _____ to.*

The Bible says God "doesn't tell _____ or change his _____. God always _____ his promises" (Num. 23:29 CEV).

DISCUSS
(25–30 minutes)

1. Paul begins with: "And my God . . ." All that follows pivots on that relationship. To claim the promise, we need to have that same connection. Describe the moment when he became *your* God.

2. In Colossians 1:27, Paul again ties together riches and glory. What does your reading of this verse add to your understanding of the promise?

> Matthew Henry ties Philippians 4:19 with the rest of the passage by writing, "As we have all things by [Christ], let us do all things for him, and to his glory."

3. How rich is God? Note what he says in Psalm 50:10–12. How does this knowledge bolster your faith that he is truly able and willing to make good on his promise to supply all your needs?

4. Note that the word translated as *in* or *by* is followed by "Christ Jesus." How does knowing that your need-supply is coming from Christ's hand challenge your day-to-day thoughts and attitudes? Your requests and behaviors?

5. While God is about the business of supplying our needs, what ought we to be doing? Take your cues from all you've learned over the course of this study.

Philippians 4:19

IMPLEMENT
(5–10 minutes)

Choose at least one activity to perform. Tell one other person which item you chose.

1. Define the true needs you have. Journal about a time when you saw God miraculously or inexplicably meet a need that you know could not have been met without his intervention. Then approach God in faith believing that he will meet your current need in his time, according to the riches he holds for you in Christ Jesus.

2. During a conversation with a fellow believer this week, bring up the subject of the glory Christ has in store for his children one day in heaven. As you talk about this hope of glory you have in Christ, note what happens to your inner joy and to the weight of earthbound challenges that have been plaguing you. Pray together, joyfully thanking God for supplying all your need—today and for eternity.

> *"As you have given to me in my distress, God will never suffer you to want without raising up help to you, as he raised you up for help to me."*
> —Adam Clarke's Commentary

WRAP UP
(5 minutes)

As this study concludes, consider all the aspects of joy that you've explored. How has your joy increased as you've learned about the joy of giving, the joy of receiving good gifts from Christ, the joy of serving, the joy of being in right relationship with Christ and his body, and the joy in difficulties and persecution? Express that joy to God and to those in your inner circle as you live your everyday life.